WILDLIFE on the FARM

WILDLIFE
on the
FARM

By Miriam Druist
Illustrated by A. Daniel Zook

Rod and Staff Publishers, Inc.
P.O. Box 3, Hwy. 172
Crockett, Kentucky 41413
Telephone: (606) 522-4348

Copyright, 1977
Rod and Staff Publishers, Inc,
Crockett, Kentucky 41413

Printed in U.S.A.

ISBN 978-07399-0101-4

Catalog no. 2475

12   13   14   15   16   —   20   19   18   17   16   15   14   13   12   11

To my husband
and sons
whose patience and presence
made these stories possible

Contents

Wildlife on the Farm

The Mallard Ducks

"Boys, boys," called Mother. "Please go to the chicken house and see if there are any eggs. I need several more for the custard I'm making."

Off ran Marlin and Mervin. Soon they came back. "We did not find any," they said.

"That's strange," said Mother. "It's three o'clock already. There should be some."

The Blairs had about a dozen chickens,

and they usually got five or six eggs a day.

Before long, Father came into the house. "Where are the boys?" he asked.

"They were just here," replied Mother. "I had sent them for eggs, and they said there weren't any. I thought that seemed a bit strange."

"Wonder if that has anything to do with the noise I heard down at the old smoke-house," said Father. "I'm going to check. Want to come along?"

Mother dried her hands and went out the back door with Father. As they came close to the smokehouse, they could see two little boys stooped down looking at something.

"What do you see, boys?" asked Father.

They both jumped up.

"We found a nest with eggs in it," said Marlin.

Father looked closer. "Why, that is a duck's nest," he said. "And it has two chicken eggs in it. How did they get there?"

Neither boy spoke for a while, and then

Mervin piped up, "We put them there before dinner."

"Well, boys, I'm afraid you spoiled the nest for the duck. She probably won't come back now. If you had left her alone, we may have had some little ducklings in our backyard."

"There's another nest under the bushes by the springhouse," said Marlin. "We saw a duck sitting there too."

"All right," said Father. "But there will be a punishment if I find any boys messing with it. Understand? If we don't bother her, we will have some ducklings. It takes about four weeks for the eggs to hatch."

Two sober boys nodded their heads.

A few weeks later, Marlin and Mervin very excitedly burst into the kitchen. "There are some little ducklings on the pond, Mother. Come and see."

Mother picked up baby Michael and went outside with the boys. There were eight ducklings swimming behind their mother.

"Let's go look at the nest by the spring-house, boys," suggested Mother.

They found an empty nest with bits of shell lying around.

Marlin dug in it a bit. He found an egg lying alone by the side of the nest. "Here's one, Mother," he said.

"That one probably didn't hatch because it wasn't under the mother duck and kept warm enough. You see, she must sit on them almost all the time and keep them warm until they are ready to hatch. That's why the nest in the old smokehouse didn't hatch. The mother was chased off and did not come back, and the eggs became cold," explained Mother.

"Next time we won't bother the duck's nest," said Mervin.

"That's right," agreed Marlin. "We like to see the little ducklings swim with their mother on the pond."

Grandpa's Visit

Marlin and Mervin were already busy playing on the floor. Mother was washing the breakfast dishes when Grandpa Blair came down the stairs into the kitchen.

Grandpa lived in another state, and Marlin and Mervin did not get to see him very often. They were happy to have Grandpa spend a few days at their house.

"Good morning, Grandpa," said Marlin.

"Good morning," echoed Mervin. "We ate our breakfast already. But there are pancakes in the oven for you."

"All right," said Grandpa.

"Did you sleep well?" asked Mervin.

"Well, there was nothing wrong with the bed, boys, but Grandpa doesn't always sleep well at night. It was very warm last night, and my lungs don't work as well as yours. I sat on the porch for a while. Then I went to bed after the air cooled off."

"What are we going to do today?" asked Marlin.

"Well, while it's cool, I think I'll fix those two gates your father has in the shop. Then when it becomes warmer, I think I'll go back and see if I can catch any fish in your stream. How about it?" asked Grandpa.

Mervin spoke up first. "We see men sitting on the bank back there, but Mother won't let us go back alone."

"If Grandpa goes, you may go along. Remember to listen and do as he says. The

water is deep in some places," reminded Mother.

To the boys, the morning seemed long. Finally, Mother called for dinner.

Mervin and Marlin soon had their plates empty. They were eager to be off.

The boys trotted up the dirt lane beside Grandpa, each carrying something. Marlin carried the line, and Mervin carried a bucket.

They sat on the bank awhile. Then Grandpa felt a tug on the line. He let Marlin and Mervin hold it for a bit to see how it felt. Then he reeled the fish in. It was a bluegill about the size of Grandpa's hand. Grandpa put some water into the bucket and dropped the fish in.

"May we go and show Mother?" asked Marlin.

"May we eat it?" asked Mervin.

"It's rather small, boys. The cat will like it though," said Grandpa.

Happily they carried the bucket to the house.

Wildlife on the Farm

"Look, Mother," chimed the boys. "Grandpa caught one small fish. He says the cat will eat it."

"Not yet, Mervin. Let's keep it awhile," suggested Marlin.

"All right," agreed Mervin.

Soon the boys became interested in something else. Then Mervin went to the kitchen for a drink. He saw the bucket on the porch, and he decided to play with the fish. He picked it out of the water and watched it flop around on the walk awhile. When it stopped, Mervin picked it up and put it back into the bucket. But it did not swim. It just floated on top of the water.

"Mother, Mother," Mervin called. "Something's wrong with the fish."

"Why, it's dead, boys. What happened?" Mother asked.

"I took it out of the bucket to play with it," said Mervin.

Mother smiled. "Then that's why it's dead. God made fish so that they can get oxygen from the water similar to the way we get oxygen from the air. You may as well call Pussy now." And they did.

Mr. Meyer's Helper

"Let's see, whose turn is it to ride with me today while I cultivate corn?" asked Father as soon as breakfast was finished.

"Mine, mine," Marlin said happily.

Mervin's face looked a little sad.

"Tomorrow will be your turn, Mervin," Mother reminded him. "If you and Michael would like something different to do, you may play with your dump trucks out on the front walk. Remember to bring them back in when you are finished with them."

Mervin smiled and nodded to Mother. Little Michael trotted along outside with him. They played nicely for a long time. Then they heard a car coming in the lane. It was Mr. Meyer, the man who owned the farm where the Blairs lived. He was going to take a broken part off the silo unloader to get it repaired. Mervin and Michael stopped their play and followed him to the barn.

Up the silo climbed Mr. Meyer. It seemed as if he were up there a long time. Finally he called down. "Stand back, boys. I'm going to push a big owl down the chute." Sure enough, down came a big gray owl. She sat dazedly on the floor. Mr. Meyer came down too.

"What happened to your hands?" asked Mervin.

"The owl attacked me as I crawled through the doorway," said Mr. Meyer. "She has a nest of sticks built up there. It has some

eggs in it. On top of the silage, I saw the fur of a rabbit, two field mice, and a half-eaten young ground hog. I guess she thought I might harm her eggs, and she wanted to protect them. Let's open the door here and let her outside now. She'll find her way back into the silo again."

"Shouldn't we kill her if she hurts people?" asked Mervin.

"No," said Mr. Meyer. "Farmers are glad for owls because they eat mice. That was a different place for a nest though. Maybe the eggs will be hatched by the time your father is ready to feed from this silo again."

"I'll have something to tell Marlin now," said Mervin. "It was his turn to ride along with Father to cultivate corn, but I think it was more fun to see that big owl."

Barn Swallow Nest

"Mother, Mother, look at this little pile of mud on the concrete. It's very hard." Marlin was helping to sweep the barn.

"Why, look up, Marlin. I believe you'll see the reason for the mud. Those two barn swallows are fussing because we are very close to the place where they are working to build a nest," said Mother.

"How long will it take them to build

their nest?" asked Marlin.

"Well, if we check each time we milk, we'll be able to watch their nest-building project. Then we will have an idea of how long it takes," said Mother.

In a few days the mother swallow stopped flying in and out of the barn window. The nest was finished, and she spent most of her time sitting on it. The father bird brought her bugs to eat sometimes. Once in a while she would leave for a short time.

Father lifted Marlin and Mervin up to look into the nest. "One, two, three, four, five eggs," the boys counted.

Finally the eggs hatched. Such a chirping noise the baby birds made as they waited their turns to be fed by mother and father swallow! The baby birds looked as if their heads were all mouths when they opened up for a bug. It seemed that they were always eating.

Slowly their fuzz was replaced by feathers. They sometimes sat on the edge of the

nest. One day a little barn swallow was pushed out. At first it started to fall, but it soon found its wings and began to fly around in the barn. By evening the nest was empty.

"Where did they go?" Marlin and Mervin wondered.

Father pointed to the electric wire by the barn. "Look up there, sons. There are some little birds sitting on the line with the bigger birds. Maybe they are the ones that left the nest we were watching. Wasn't it nice that we could watch the barn swallows so closely?"

"Yes," chorused the boys. "We're glad God made barn swallows."

The Water Snake

It was a beautiful, balmy Sunday afternoon. The Yoder family was visiting the Blairs.

"May we go outside?" asked Marlin.

Mother glanced at Sister Yoder. Sister Yoder nodded yes.

"I suppose you may," said Mother. "But please remember that Stanley, Suzann, and Marlene aren't used to being around water.

So be careful and don't push or shove."

Happy noises floated through the open window for a while. Then some excited shouts filled the air.

"A snake, a snake!" yelled Stanley.

Mother and Sister Yoder went out to the back yard.

"A snake was lying along the edge of the stream," said Marlin. "When we yelled, it went away—fast. That's the second one we saw since we live here."

"Snakes, ugh!" said Suzann. "I'll play inside."

"That's where the other one was," stated Mervin.

"What?" chorused the Yoder children in one breath.

"That's right children," said Mother. "One morning we came in from the barn and saw one lying in the spring water in the fruit cellar. It did scare us a bit. But as soon as it heard noise, it disappeared under the wall. We have never seen it inside since.

"Father says they are much like the garter snake, only larger. About thirty inches long, I think. They are not poisonous, and they help to complete the balance of nature. They destroy mice, insects, and other pests. They usually slip quickly out of sight. God planned something even for the snakes to do. So it's best to avoid them and kill them only when they might endanger us."

"I still don't like snakes," said Suzann.

"Not many people do," said Sister Yoder. "But they do have a place in God's creation. And we must be careful about the poisonous ones. But God has something for snakes to do too."

A Skunk Story

Marlin pressed his nose against the damp window. He watched the rain splash against the car and run in small streams down its side.

"Boys," Mother said, "you'll need to find something to do inside."

For a while they played with Play-Doh but became bored with that. Then Mervin suggested, "Let's play with the Tinkertoys."

Wildlife on the Farm

After a while, Marlin asked, "Mother, please tell us stories while you're ironing."

"All right," said Mother. "I'll tell you about an animal we have seen only once since we moved to this farm. Can you guess what it is?"

"Raccoon?" asked Mervin.

"No," said Mother.

"Skunk?" asked Marlin.

"Right," said Mother. "A skunk story, and Marlin is in it too. Do you remember, Marlin?"

Marlin nodded.

"One evening while Father and Mother were milking, Marlin decided to walk out the lane. We lived at Woodsboro then, and Grandmother Wilson lived at the end of the lane. Marlin liked to ride his tricycle there. When Marlin came to the bridge that went across the little stream in the lane, he stopped and looked. There was a black cat and five babies drinking by the edge of the water. When the cat saw Marlin, she started toward him, all

her babies following. Marlin became frightened because a cat and kittens had never followed him before. The faster Marlin walked, the faster the cat walked. Marlin began to cry, and Grandmother heard him. She saw a strange sight when she stepped out the back doorway. There was Marlin running as fast as his two-year-old legs could carry him with a mother skunk and five little ones right behind. When Grandmother shouted, the skunk and her babies ran into the tall grass in the meadow.

"Then Grandmother called Father and asked if he had a gun. We couldn't imagine why she needed a gun. Then she told us. Father went out to the meadow and looked for them, but he could not see them anywhere. He was ready to put the gun away when he saw something moving in the carrot row in the garden behind our house. The skunk family were on their way back home— under the chicken house. But they didn't make it. Father killed them all. God made skunks to help balance nature too. But because these were close to the house, Father killed them so that they would not eat the eggs out of the chicken house and so that you boys wouldn't get sprayed."

"Aunt Marsha Lee was sprayed one time when she was helping Brother Herrs," spoke up Marlin.

"That's right," said Mother. "She said the whole house smelled like a skunk till she had washed everything."

"I'm glad we don't have skunks close to our house here," said Mervin.

"So am I," laughed Mother.

Visitors and the Fox

The Blair family were just finishing their supper when Tammy started barking.

"Someone is here," said Marlin.

"I hope it's visitors," said Mervin.

"You may turn on the porch light," said Mother, looking toward Marlin.

Marlin jumped off his chair and turned the switch. Mervin opened the door.

To be sure, it was visitors! Marlin and

Mervin were always happy when Paul Martin's came because they had two boys about their ages—Benjamin and Timothy. Then there was baby Judith, who was about Michael's age.

"Come in, come in," chimed the two oldest Blair boys.

The Martin boys called back, "Come out, come out."

"Mother, they want us to come outside," said Marlin.

Father and Mother went to the door.

Paul said, "I have something here the boys might want to see."

They all went outside. There by Paul's car lay a full-grown red fox.

"He ran across the knoll in the lane as we came in," said Paul. "I could not avoid hitting him."

"Is that the one we saw in the hayfield this summer?" asked Marlin.

"Probably," said Father.

"I don't like foxes," said Mervin. "I'm afraid they might eat me."

"This one won't, Mervin," said Paul. "He's dead, very dead."

"I think foxes are shy of people, Mervin. You need not be afraid of them. You'll probably never get this close to a live fox. Since this one is dead, wouldn't you like to touch his fur?" asked Father.

"No," said Mervin. He stood a little ways away from the rest of the group, with his hands behind his back.

Slowly, Mervin inched toward the rest. He stood beside his father for a while. At last he stooped to touch the fox. "Why, Father," he said, "God made the fox's hair a lot like Tammy's. If I stand beside you, I'm not afraid."

"That's good," said Father. "That's the way God wants us to feel when we stay close to Him. 'Be not afraid.'"

The New Pet

"I'm going to the store for a few things," said Mother one afternoon. "Anyone want to ride along?"

"Not me," said Mervin.

"Not me," echoed Marlin.

Father was working in the shop. "I can keep Michael also if you want me to. I'll be around the buildings until the feed truck comes," said Father.

"All right," agreed Mother. "It should not take me very long."

Mervin and Marlin rode their tricycles. Little Michael played in the sandbox.

Soon they heard the sound of a big truck. It was the feed truck. Tammy began to bark. Father called her, but she ran to the bend in the lane. Just as the truck rounded the curve, Tammy jumped out, barking. The back wheels caught her, and she fell into the lane, dead.

When Mother came home, Marlin and Mervin were close to tears.

"That bad feed man killed Tammy," burst out Mervin.

"Well, boys, it wasn't the feed man's fault. Tammy had a bad habit of chasing cars and trucks. It was her own fault. We tried to teach her, but she chased cars and trucks before we got her. The habit was hard to break. That's why Father and Mother try to help you break bad habits while you are young. Habits can be good, and we like that kind.

But anything that we do over and over that is unkind, untruthful, or harmful must be broken.

"As for Tammy, she's dead. Maybe if we watch the advertisements, we can find another dog."

Within a few days, Father found some people who had a puppy for sale.

Marlin and Mervin were happy with Scotty, and they were determined to help him learn good habits while he was young.

The Rabbit Family

"Boys," said Mother, "I am going to mow the back lawn now. Please move your toys to the front porch. It isn't safe for you to play close to where I am mowing."

"All right," answered Marlin as he and his brothers prepared to move their toys farther from the spot where Mother was going to work.

Mother started the mower and began her

job. "I surely hope this mower runs all right today," she thought to herself. The last time she had tried to mow, she was only half finished when the mower stopped running. The grass in the back yard was rather long. It was going to take a while to finish the job.

Mother had made two trips around the yard when she noticed that some fur had come out from under the mower. She stopped to investigate, and shivered a bit to herself as she noticed a depression in the ground by her right foot. "Probably a mouse nest," she mused to herself. The boys would enjoy seeing that too; so she stopped the mower.

Before she could call to them, Mervin came running. "Are you finished already, Mother?" he asked.

"No," Mother answered, "but I found something you boys might like to see. Go tell Marlin and Michael to come."

Soon three little boys were kneeling by Mother in the grass. She reached toward the

little hole in the ground and pulled back
some dead grass. Next was a layer of fur.
Carefully she pulled that back too. To the
surprise of them all, it was not a mouse nest
but a nest of bunnies. There were seven or
eight of them. They were still very tiny. They
did not have very much fur, and their eyes
were not open yet.

"Let's cover them up again so that the
cats cannot find them. Maybe in a few days
we will check on them again," said Mother.

A few days later, the family examined the
nest. The mother rabbit had been back. The
little bunnies were growing more fur, and
their eyes were open. Two of them tried to
jump out of the nest. Quickly Mother put
them back in; out they jumped again.

"Marlin, go and get a basket. We'll put
that over the nest until dark."

Quickly Marlin scampered off and was
soon back.

"We don't want the cats to find the bunnies. And they are too young to be on their

own," Mother explained. She turned the basket over the nest. With backward glances, they walked quietly away.

Over the weekend, the Blair family visited some friends in another state. The first thing the boys thought of when they got back home on Monday was the nest of bunnies.

Yes, they were still there, and the hole was so full of growing bunnies that a bulge could be seen on top of the ground. They were still covered with grass and fur.

As Mother carefully pulled back the covering for the boys to see, bunnies ran everywhere—under the peony bushes, under the chicken house, under the pine trees. "O Father," called Mother, "come help me catch these bunnies!"

Father laughed, and said, "If they left home that fast, I believe they can take care of themselves."

Later in the week, Mother went to the garden to cut some lettuce for dinner.

Mervin went with her. As Mother reached

into the lettuce, she felt something soft. In an instant, a little bunny appeared, and then hopped out of sight.

"O Mother," gasped Mervin, "was that one of our little bunnies?"

"We cannot be sure, son," Mother answered, "but it is nice to imagine that it was. We won't miss a little lettuce, will we? Just think how well God cares for the bunnies."

"And He cares for us too," said Mervin softly to himself.

The Turtle

"A delivery man brought us something today. Anyone want to guess what it is?" asked Mother at the supper table one balmy spring evening.

But no one could think what might have come that excited Mother so much.

"Why, the man brought our red raspberry plants. Isn't that nice!" exclaimed Mother.

"Already?" asked Father in surprise. "We ordered them just last week."

"I was surprised too," said Mother. "I put them down in the springhouse. Do you think we could plant them after supper this evening?"

"I believe so," said Father. "How many willing helpers will we have?"

"Me, me, me," answered three happy voices.

"Good," said Father, "I'm sure we will all enjoy helping to eat them too. While Mother clears away the supper, you boys may get the water hose, a shovel, and the berry plants and carry them to the bank at the edge of the garden. That is where we want to plant them."

Eager hands went to work. The idea of nice, fresh, sweet berries to eat made the boy's jobs seem like play.

"I'm glad we worked this bank last week," said Mother. "It seems nice and mellow now."

The Turtle

"Yes," remarked Father, "and with this thick layer of sawdust, I don't think we should have much trouble with weeds."

"May I dig the holes?" asked Marlin.

"You may try, son," said Father. "We need twelve holes about this far apart." Father measured with his shovel handle to show Marlin the correct distance.

Just as Marlin began to dig the third hole, he said, "Look at this pretty stone. Oh! Oh! It's moving!"

"That looks like a box turtle," said Father. "See, it was digging itself into the sawdust. Perhaps it was going to lay some eggs. Turtles usually live close to water. But when it's time to lay eggs, they choose some high, dry spot. After the eggs are laid in the hole that they dig with their back feet, they leave, and probably never see the baby turtles. The eggs are hatched by the warm sunshine. Sometimes enemies find the eggs and eat them before they hatch."

"Will she lay eggs here in the raspberry

bed?" asked Mervin.

"We've probably disturbed her now," said Father.

"Will she snap us?" asked Michael.

"That is not a snapping turtle," said Father. "See how it looks like a stone. All the feet and the head are drawn inside. A snapping turtle cannot draw its head inside the shell."

"The Russel boys found two snapping turtles," said Marlin. "People eat them. They said a snapping turtle's head will snap after the head is cut off from the rest of the body."

"That's right. A snapping turtle would not make a good pet," said Father.

Feeding the Deer

"How would you boys like to visit the zoo on Marlin's birthday?" asked Father one evening.

"When's Marlin's birthday?" asked Mervin.

"In three days, son," answered Mother.

"Oh, goody, goody," they all chorused.

"Well, we will plan for a trip to the zoo, unless something else would come up," said Father.

Wildlife on the Farm

The evening before Marlin's birthday, Father said, "Boys, it looks as if it will rain before tomorrow is over. I have one field of corn to cultivate yet, and I feel that should be done before we take a day off. I think we should plan our zoo trip for another day."

Three sad-faced boys nodded their heads. "Could we go the next day?" asked Marlin.

"The next day is Saturday. It would be rather late until we get home in the evening. We do not want to plan to do something that would make us extra tired on the Lord's Day. We will go sometime, but this time it did not work out as I had thought," explained Father.

Mother had a smile on her face, and the boys saw her wink at Father.

"Perhaps I can think of something special to do close home," suggested Mother.

"Fine," agreed Father.

"What is it?" asked Mervin.

"I'll save that for a surprise. After you

boys finish all your little jobs in the house tomorrow, I'll tell you," said Mother.

Three excited boys got ready for bed.

The next morning Mervin woke up first.

"Marlin, Marlin," he called. "Today is your birthday; wake up. Today is the day for our surprise."

Soon Marlin and Michael were up and dressed too. After breakfast one boy dried the dishes, one boys swept the kitchen floor, and one picked up the toys in the playroom.

Finally Mother said, "Well, I believe everything is finished now. You boys wash your hands and comb your hair. Then you may get into the car."

At the end of the lane, Mother turned left. "We are going to Mapleville," she said. "Does anyone want to guess what we are going to do?"

"We are going to the park," said Marlin.

"Right," said Mother. "We have often driven past and seen the deer there. Today we are going to stop and feed them. The deer are tame and they eat corn out of your hands. There is also an ice cream stand there. I will get each of you a cone before we leave. How is that for a birthday surprise, Marlin?" asked Mother.

"It is a nice surprise. Thank you, Mother," said Marlin.

"What is in that bag?" asked Mervin as they got out of the car.

"I brought an ear of corn along," said Mother.

Three happy boys dashed here and there, counting and watching and feeding the deer.

While they were eating the cones Mother had bought for them, Michael walked up to the fence. As quick as a flash, one deer's tongue reached out and licked off the top of his cone. "Mother," he squealed, "deer eat ice cream too!"

Later, on the way home, Marlin said, "Mother, I was a little disappointed that we could not go to the zoo, but this was fun too."

"Yes, I know, son," said Mother. "We

should always remember to say 'if the Lord will' when we make plans. Disappointments come to grownups too. It's better if we do not become too set on doing things. Let's always try to remember to include God's will in our planning."

The Baby Robin

"Mervin, Mervin, where are you?" called Marlin.

"Coming," answered Mervin. "What do you want?"

"Look what I found in the grass under the pine trees." Marlin held out his right hand.

"A baby bird! What kind is it?" gasped Mervin.

"I think it must be a robin. Look here

under its wing. The feathers are brownish orange. Let's go ask Mother," said Marlin.

The boys found Mother in the kitchen, baking cookies. "Look what I found," said Marlin. "Can you tell us what kind of a baby bird this is, Mother?"

"Why, I believe it is a robin, boys," said Mother. "Where did you find it?"

"Under the pine trees," said Marlin. "May we keep it for a pet?"

"I'm afraid it will die indoors, boys," said Mother. "But you may try to feed it. Go get my hand spade and dig up some worms in the garden. Here is a can; you may put them into it. The little bird probably fell from its nest in the pine tree."

Soon several worms were wiggling around in the can. Marlin held the bird loosely in his hand. Mervin dug a worm out of the can and dangled it over the baby robin's head.

No response.

Mother gently stroked the underside of the little bird's neck. Instantly the tiny

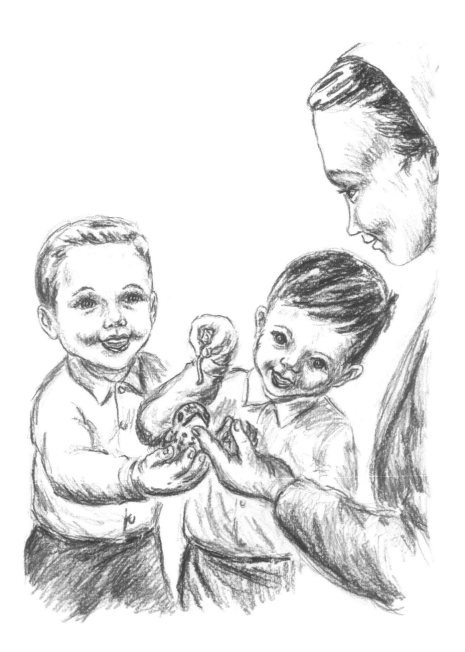

mouth opened, then closed again.

"Now," instructed Mother, "the next time I do that, you drop the worm inside quickly, Mervin."

Mervin held the worm close to the robin's mouth. Mother rubbed the little neck. That worm disappeared in the tiny red throat. A few more worms disappeared in the same way. Then the little robin would not open its mouth any more.

"I think it's full now, boys. It is not used to being fed so fast. It takes a while for the mother bird to find worms sometimes, and there is more than one little bird in the nest to feed. Let's set the baby robin on a branch in the pine tree. Look up there. I wonder if that is the mother robin. She sure is scolding about something." The boys looked in the direction Mother was pointing.

"May we feed it again?" asked Marlin.

"Perhaps we can try again before bed-time," said Mother.

The next day the boys fed the little bird

three times. The last time it stretched its wings and fluttered from Marlin's hand. Mother caught it and set it back on a branch in the pine tree.

"Don't be surprised if it's gone tomorrow morning, boys. Its wings seemed almost strong enough to fly," said Mother.

The next morning, the spot where the little robin had sat was empty. But Marlin and Mervin were glad for the privilege they had had to see one of God's beautiful birds so closely.

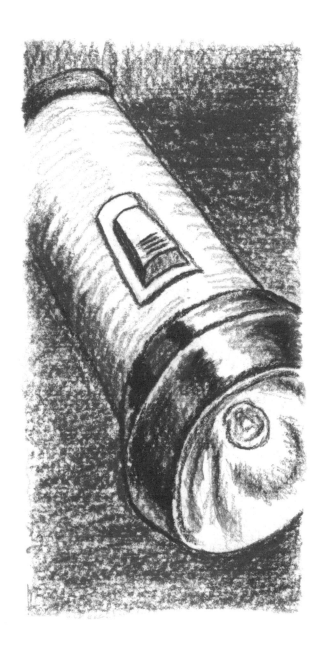

Eyes in the Dark

"What are you going to do, Mother?" asked Mervin when he noticed the picnic basket sitting on the kitchen table.

"Pack a picnic supper, son," replied Mother. "We decided to take Grandpa Blair home this evening so that Father can mow hay tomorrow if the weather is clear."

"You mean we are going to Somerset tonight? Who will milk our cows?" asked

Wildlife on the Farm

Marlin.

"Father will milk early. We plan to leave at six o'clock. We will eat our supper on the way. We should reach Grandpa's place about eight o'clock. Lord willing, we should be climbing into our beds about eleven o'clock," said Mother.

"Oh, this will be fun," said Marlin. "May we take some pillows and covers along?"

"Surely," said Mother. "I'll fix a place on the floor for one of you. The other two can lie on the seat."

Before long the chores were finished. Grandpa packed everything he had brought into his suitcase. With a grin he reached into his pocket and then gave each boy a piece of candy. "That's for being good while I was here," he said.

"Thank you," chorused the boys. "Come back again sometime. We are glad to have you with us."

Mother carried the picnic basket out to the car. Each boy carried a pillow. Grandpa

put his suitcase into the trunk. Last of all, Father came out of the house. He carried a flashlight.

"Why do we need a flashlight?" asked Mervin.

"We might have a flat tire," said Father. His eyes twinkled.

"Do you really think so?" asked Marlin.

"I hope not," said Father. "We may find another need for it."

The boys looked at each other in a puzzled way, but no one said a word.

The car turned westward, and soon the family was munching on Mother's tasty egg-salad sandwiches. They watched a beautiful sunset in the west as they traveled.

"Isn't it marvelous that we can watch the same sunset at home, boys," said Father. "Just look at those brilliant colors."

Slowly the colors faded away. The sky was growing darker.

At last they reached Grandpa's house. Father helped him carry his things inside.

Wildlife on the Farm

After a little while, Father announced, "We must start home again." Good-nights were exchanged, and the little family turned homeward.

"Look at all the stars that came out while we were inside," said Mother. "It must be nearly a full moon tonight. What a beautiful night sky."

Before long the boys were beginning to nestle down on pillows. "Cover me, Mother," said Michael.

"Are you going to sleep already?" asked Father. "We will soon be crossing the mountain. Maybe I'll get a chance to use my flashlight."

"Just keep watching out the windows," said Mother.

Before long, Father began to slow down. He pulled off the road and stopped the car. Then he pointed to the clearing in the valley just below them. Sure enough! Sixteen deer were grazing in the beautiful moonlight. Father reached for his flashlight. Sixteen heads jerked to attention. For a few moments, many shining eyes gleamed like tiny lights in their direction. Then, as if someone had given a signal, they all gracefully bounded away into the dark shadows of the woods beyond them.

"Is that why you wanted to bring your flashlight, Father?" asked Mervin.

"Yes," said Father. "I have seen deer here before. I was hoping you boys would get a chance to see them too. Of course, it would also be handy to have a flashlight along if we did have car trouble. But let us trust God to take us home safely."

Honey Bees

Father dialed 762-7375 by memory. That was the telephone number of Peter Dean's, the Blairs' closest neighbors.

"Good morning," said Father when Peter answered the telephone. "May I borrow your dump truck today? I would like to move some big rocks out of the back field."

"Surely," replied Peter. "You may use it

the rest of the week if you like. I won't be needing it."

"Thanks very much, Peter. We will be over to get it. Good-bye."

"I guess you'll have to ride along, Mother, so that you can drive the car home," said Father.

Marlin, Mervin, and Michael grabbed their caps and headed for the car. Mother hurried to get her purse, and soon they were on their way.

Just as they rounded a curve in the Deans' lane, they noticed Peter all dressed up with coveralls, gloves, and a net down over his hat. He was bent over two white boxes under a walnut tree.

"What is Peter doing?" asked Mervin.

"Those are bee boxes," said Marlin.

"I think he is getting ready to take some honey off," said Father. "Shall we stop and watch him?"

"Yes, let's do," said the boys.

"What is in that bucket?" asked Marlin.

"I believe that is what he uses to smoke the bees. It is a burlap bag that he has started afire. Watch," said Father. "He holds it close to the hive and the bees quit buzzing."

Carefully Peter pushed the bees off the sides of the hive with a scraper. They fell to the ground as if they were dead.

Peter raised the white box up. Inside were many smaller boxes of honey. Those were what Peter wanted. He took out the small boxes of honey and leaned them against the walnut tree. Then he put the white box back into place.

Picking up the smoking bucket in one hand and the honey in the other, he headed for the house. "Come along," he called to the Blairs.

"Have you ever been stung while gathering honey?" asked Father a little while later.

"Only once," replied Peter. "I guess I hadn't smoked them long enough. After you get to know bees well enough, you can tell if they are going to sting. They make a special high-pitched buzzing sound."

"It surely is a miracle how those little creatures can make honey, isn't it?" said Father.

"Yes," Peter agreed. "I find them very interesting to watch."

Then turning to the boys with a smile, Peter asked, "How would you like to take two little boxes of honey along home to taste?"

"Oh, goody," said Marlin and Mervin. "We would really like that."

High Water

"Mother, when is the rain going to stop?" asked Mervin anxiously.

"I don't know, son, but it looks as though it could rain all day," replied Mother.

"Do you know what the milkman told Father?" asked Marlin.

"No, what?" asked Mother.

"He said all the roads which cross the river north of us, up to Curtisville, are closed.

The water is over the bridges. Do you think we'll have a flood, Mother?" asked Marlin.

"There may be a flood in this area," replied Mother, "but who knows what the Bible says about floods?"

"I think it says the earth will never all be covered with water at one time again," answered Marlin.

"That's right," said Mother. "What special sign did God give us, Mervin?"

"The rainbow," said Mervin. "Will we see a rainbow when it stops raining?"

"Perhaps we will," said Mother.

"The water is still rising," announced Father after the milkman left. "Have you checked the cellar lately?" asked Father looking at Mother.

"Yes," answered Mother. "I was wondering if we should move the canned fruit up higher."

"I'll go down and see," said Father.

Soon hurried steps were heard coming back up the cellar steps. Father pulled off his

boots and headed for the telephone. "I am going to call Mr. Meyer, the landlord. The water is almost covering the concrete platform on which the furnace sits," Father announced.

A half hour later Mr. and Mrs. Meyer came driving in the lane.

"That sure is a lot of water, boys. Did you do any fishing yet?" asked Mr. Meyer.

Mr. Meyer and Father put on their boots and waded through the cellar. Mr. Meyer turned off the furnace and shut off the gas line leading into it. "The weatherman calls for clearing this afternoon; so perhaps the water will soon reach its peak," said Mr. Meyer.

Meanwhile, the fishing question gave Marlin and Mervin an idea. They pulled on their boots and asked Mother for a jar.

"What are you going to do?" asked Mother.

"See if we can catch some minnows in the cellar," said Mervin.

"Isn't the water too cloudy?" asked Mother.

"We'll see," said the boys.

"Say, boys," said Mr. Meyer when he saw the jar, "we saw a small crab here a little while ago. Maybe I can find him for you."

"Oh, good," said Marlin. "I would like to take it to school."

Soon Mr. Crab was a captive in a jar.

"Look, what is that?" shouted Mervin excitedly.

Father and Mr. Meyer looked in the direction that Mervin had pointed. They saw an orange flash in the water.

"Now what we need is a strainer with a long handle," said Father. "Then Marlin would have two things to take along to school."

They lost sight of the orange flash and had almost given up seeing it again, when Father saw it swim by his boot. Quickly he scooped down into the water around his feet.

"Well, I believe you have yourself a salamander now, Marlin," said Mr. Meyer. "You

can have a real exhibit at school tomorrow."
When Mr. Meyer, Father, and the boys
returned to the kitchen, where Mrs. Meyer
and Mother were visiting, everyone seemed
to notice at once that the rain had almost
stopped and that the sun was just beginning
to peek through the clouds.

"Now, let's watch for a rainbow," said
Mervin.

A Quiet Visit

"Wake up, boys," called Mother one Sunday evening. "Father and I are finished with the chores. We have decided to go visit Grandfather's. I'm laying out the clothes you shall wear, and you dress while I put supper on the table."

"I'm still sleepy," mumbled Mervin.

"Aw, come on. I'll race you getting dressed," urged Marlin.

"That's not fair 'cause I can't tie my shoes yet, and my buttons get all mixed," Mervin objected.

"You work at it, Mervin," said Mother. "I'll be back up after I'm finished putting supper on the table. I'll tie your shoes and help you to button your shirt. I'll dress little Michael then too."

Soon everyone was dressed. Father asked the blessing on the evening meal, and three hungry boys made supper disappear fast. They liked to go visit Grandfather's.

"Now listen, boys," said Father while they were riding in the car. "Grandfather hasn't been home from the hospital very long, and he still tires easily. You must remember to play quietly."

"What can we do then?" asked Marlin, who liked to ride tricycle in Grandfather's basement.

"I'm sure Grandmother has coloring books and crayons," Mother said. "Maybe you can sing some songs for them. And perhaps

each of you can say a verse you learned in Sunday school."

"Did you bring a songbook?" asked Father as they pulled into the driveway.

"Yes, and it looks as though we might even have some help to sing. Whose car is that?" asked Mother.

"I believe it's Uncle Joel's," said Father. "Now remember to play quietly, boys. We must not stay too long either, or our visit will do more harm than good."

"All right," promised the boys.

Grandfather's face lit up as the little family walked in. "I'm glad someone came to spend the evening," he said. "Joel's are getting ready to leave."

"Oh, already?" asked Mother. "We brought a songbook along. Can you stay long enough to help us sing a few songs?"

"Yes, do that," said Grandmother. "We would enjoy that."

"Yes, sing," said Grandfather too.

First Uncle Joel's children and Marlin

and Mervin sang several Sunday school songs. The grownups each chose a song too. Then Uncle Joel's went home.

Father and Mother sat down to visit with Grandfather and Grandmother, and the boys played quietly in the kitchen.

About eight-thirty, Father said, "Put your toys away, boys. It is time to go home."

"Thank you for the visit and for singing for me!" exclaimed Grandfather.

"Good-bye, good-bye," chorused Marlin and Mervin.

"Good-bye," called Grandfather and Grandmother.

"Thank you for being quiet and obedient," Father told the boys on the way home. "Grandfather really enjoyed the visit because you played quietly and helped to sing."

"We enjoyed it too, didn't we, Mervin?" said Marlin smiling.

"We sure did!" Mervin echoed.

Marlin Learns a Lesson

Marlin and Stanley jumped out of the car, swinging their lunch pails. "I'm really glad you could come home with me!" exclaimed Marlin as they ran up the walk.

"I am too," Stanley said, puffing.

Mother met them at the door. "Good evening, boys. Come in. How was school today?" asked Mother.

"Fine," answered Marlin. "See, I have a

smiling face on my numbers paper."

"I have one too," added Stanley.

"I'm hungry, Mother. What may we eat?" asked Marlin.

"There are apples on the back porch. Get one for each of you. You may eat them here in the kitchen. Then, Marlin, change into your old clothes, and you boys may help me unload the corn in the grain wagon. Father needs to work in the corncrib to level the corn."

"Oh, good, good," chorused the boys. "That will be fun."

Mother left the house and began to help Father. When she was about half finished, she saw the boys coming across the lawn. Stanley had on an old sweater of Marlin's. Marlin had on his barn jacket. They ran toward the grain wagon. Stanley jumped into the wagon first, and Marlin followed. As Marlin swung his leg over the edge, Mother noticed he was still wearing brown trousers— his school ones.

"Marlin," called Mother above the noise of the corn falling into the elevator, "you didn't change your trousers. Go back into the house, and do as I said."

"But, Mother, the wagon will be empty till I get back out," he said.

"I'm sorry, Marlin, but if you had obeyed promptly, you could stay and help. Go, now," said Mother.

With tears in his eyes, Marlin started for the house.

When Marlin came back, the wagon was empty. "Finished?" he asked.

"Yes," said Stanley. "Let's play ball now."

"All right," agreed Marlin. His face looked happier. But the boys had to hunt and hunt for the ball. Finally they found it under some shrubbery.

Each boy had a few turns kicking it. Then Stanley heard his father coming in the back field lane.

"Oh, must you go so soon? We didn't get to play very long," said Marlin.

"Why, Marlin," said Mother kindly, "Stanley has been here over an hour. But because you didn't promptly change your school clothes and because you didn't put your ball away last evening when I reminded you, a lot of time was wasted. Wouldn't it be better to obey promptly? Then you'd have more time."

"Yes, Mother," said Marlin. "The next time I'll try to remember to be prompt. Then I'll have more time to play."

Marlin's Red Pencil Case

"Mother," Marlin said one evening. "May I have a pencil case? Stephanie has a blue one. Kenny and Floyd have green ones. Lyle has a brown one, and Joellen's is yellow. May I use Father's?"

"O Marlin," said Mother. "Father has had that wooden pencil case since he was in first grade. His father got that for him years ago. I guess it is rather special to him. Just be patient and wait a bit longer."

One day a catalog came in the mail. In it was pictured a red pencil case. "Just the thing for Marlin," thought Mother. "I'll surprise him," So Mother ordered the little red case and six pencils with Marlin's name printed on them. There were a ruler, a pencil sharpener, and an eraser in the case too.

A few weeks passed. One day the mailman brought a package for Marlin. His face broke into a happy smile when he saw what was in the package. His very own pencil case.

"Oh, thank you, Mother. I'm really glad there's a ruler. Yesterday the first graders were supposed to draw houses, and my roof got very lopsided. And the pencils even have my name on them. I will try to keep this case nice for a long time like Father did."

"Let's take out all the pencils but two, and keep them in the desk drawer," suggested Mother. "After all, you can't use them all at once. With two, you'll have a spare if a point breaks. When they are used up, you

may have two more."

A little cloud passed over Marlin's happy face. But he agreed, "Okay, Mother."

The next morning Mother discovered something that made her very sad. Two of Marlin's pencils were missing.

That evening when Marlin came home, Mother greeted him as usual at the door. "How was school today, Marlin?" asked Mother.

"Oh, fine," said Marlin, not looking at Mother.

"Marlin, I want you to bring your pencil case home tomorrow evening," said Mother.

"Why?" asked Marlin.

"You know why, don't you, Marlin?" asked Mother softly.

"Yes." Marlin's chin quivered. "It has too many pencils in it."

"That's right, Marlin. And because you were dishonest and deceitful, you will have to bring your new red pencil case home and leave it here for two weeks," said Mother.

Wildlife on the Farm

"Oh, how long will that be?" asked Marlin.

"Let's mark it on the calendar," suggested Mother. "A black x for each day you must leave it home. Perhaps this will help you to remember the importance of being honest and true."

"I'm sure it will. Now I have to wait two weeks longer to use my little red pencil case," agreed Marlin.

"It is never right to be dishonest, son. Even if no one would find it out, God would know, and in our own hearts we would know it too," said Mother. "I hope my little boy has learned a lesson he'll never forget."

144

The Trapper

A fresh blanket of snow had fallen during the night. Marlin, Mervin, and Michael were happy and excited about riding on their new toboggan. While they ate their breakfast, they chatted about where they would ride.

Suddenly Scotty began to bark. Then the boys saw a red jeep in the driveway.

"Who is that, Father?" asked Marlin.

"He is a trapper. He came while you

were at school yesterday and asked if he could set some traps along the stream," replied Father. "He is probably here to check them now."

"That would be interesting to watch," said Marlin. "May we go with him?"

"I guess I could go along with you. We will bed and feed the heifers after he leaves. But dress warmly. It is very cold outside this morning," said Father.

No one needed to be told the second time. Jackets, hoods, gloves, and boots were pulled on in a hurry.

A cold blast of air entered the kitchen as the three boys followed Father out into the newly fallen snow. Mother stood at the door and watched them walk down the lane toward the stream.

The man was already bent over the first trap, examining it. Carefully he lifted a muskrat. And another. And another. Once he came upon a trapped opossum. One trap had a raccoon that had probably come to the

stream to wash his food and had gotten his
paws caught.

Then the boys heard a whistle of surprise.

"What now, Father?" asked Marlin.

"Trouble?" called Father to the trapper.

"No, surprise," answered the man. "I've
got a mink. They are rather rare in this
area."

After the man finished checking, unload-
ing, and resetting the rest of the traps, he
headed back toward the jeep, stopping along
the bank to pick up his catch. The boys
helped him carry the muskrats to the jeep.

"I think I made a pretty good catch this
time, Mr. Blair," said the trapper. "That's
nineteen muskrats, an opossum, a raccoon,
and a mink."

"Which is worth the most?" asked
Father.

"That mink pelt will be the most valuable.
Then the raccoon and muskrat. The opossum
isn't worth much at all. Years ago you could
make a living trapping in the winter, but now

Wildlife on the Farm

man-made furs have changed all of that. I still like to get out on these beautiful winter mornings, and most farmers are glad enough to get rid of these pesky muskrats that dig up the stream banks.

"See, boys, I know which animals made these tracks through the fresh snow. Those are the coon's tracks there. That's rabbit tracks there by the bushes. Up across the hill are fox's tracks. Here are different bird prints. They were hopping around these bushes and eating berries," explained the trapper.

As Father and the boys walked back to the house, they talked about the different kinds of animals that God had created, and their habits. They also talked about how God provides food for the animals and birds even during the long, cold winter.

"Yes, boys, God notices if one sparrow falls to the ground. How much better He cares for us," said Father reverently.